Original title:
Evergreen Giggles

Copyright © 2025 Creative Arts Management OÜ
All rights reserved.

Author: Clara Whitfield
ISBN HARDBACK: 978-1-80567-331-6
ISBN PAPERBACK: 978-1-80567-630-0

Whirling with the Wind

A gusty breeze spins around,
Tickling toes from the ground.
Dandelions bounce with cheer,
Chasing laughter far and near.

Squirrels dance like little clowns,
Nutty giggles swirl in towns.
Branches sway, they twist and shout,
Nature joins the joyful bout.

Mirthful Moments in the Trees

Up above where branches sway,
Chirpy birds have much to say.
Acorn caps become the hats,
Plump little mice wear them like mats.

Sunlight peeks through leafy screens,
Frolicking in the golden sheens.
Joyful giggles rise and fall,
Nature's laughter, hear it call.

The Playful Palette of Nature

In gardens bright with colors bold,
Cheerful daisies tell their old.
Brushes dipped in laughter's hue,
Paint the skies with grin or two.

Butterflies join the vibrant dance,
Wings a-flutter, they take a chance.
Petals giggle, soft and light,
Nature's palette, pure delight.

Laughter Between the Leaves

Whispers float on breezy trails,
Friendly banter like veiled tales.
Leaves shake hands with joyful glee,
Sharing smiles from tree to tree.

Down below the playful poke,
Bouncing ants in funny cloak.
Underneath a giggling limb,
Nature hums, a cheerful hymn.

The Dance of the Daisies

In the meadow, daisies sway,
Bouncing around, they steal the day.
Tiny critters join the spree,
Laughing loudly, wild and free.

Breezes tickle, petals twirl,
Jumping jigs make flowers unfurl.
Bees are buzzing, joining in,
What a party, let's begin!

Sunlight glimmers, shadows play,
Who needs worries? Not today!
Every bloom wears a big grin,
Nature's dance, let the fun begin!

As the evening sun dips low,
Daisies wave, their faces glow.
With a giggle, they take a bow,
Tomorrow's fun is waiting now!

Whistling Woods and Whimsy

In the woods, where whispers sing,
Squirrels chatter, and bluebirds swing.
Branches sway with playful cheer,
Nature's laughter rings out clear.

Trees wear hats of leafy green,
While raccoons dance, a funny scene.
Breezes toss the acorns around,
Laughter echoes, a joyous sound.

Mushrooms caper, sprouting tall,
As bunnies join the quirky ball.
Every critter, every bug,
In the forest, shared the hug.

When the moon begins to rise,
Fireflies twinkle, bright as eyes.
Whistling woods, a quirky thrill,
With giggles echoing, time stands still!

Roaming the Resplendent Realm

Through the fields of colors bright,
Wandering souls find pure delight.
Bubbly streams and sparkly stones,
 Everywhere, joy freely groans.

Hopping frogs play leap and chase,
 Smiling flowers set the pace.
 Every step a joyful cheer,
In this land, there's naught to fear.

Clouds fluff up like cotton candy,
 While hills roll, oh so dandy.
Laughter dances, tickles the air,
In this realm, fun is everywhere.

As twilight wraps the day in peace,
 The giggles linger, never cease.
 Roaming freely, hearts aglow,
 In this world, we freely flow!

Frolics Under the Verdant Shade

Beneath the leaves, we play and cheer,
A squirrel steals snacks, we laugh, oh dear!
With every jump, and twist, and turn,
The laughter flies, like leaves that churn.

A picnic spread, but ants are bold,
They march right in, our food to hold!
We chase them off with silly shouts,
In nature's game, we jump about.

Joyful Echoes in the Glade

The tree trunks hum a silly tune,
As shadows dance beneath the moon.
We play at tag, our giggles rise,
A boisterous scene beneath the skies.

With every leap, our spirits soar,
A bouncy ball rolls from the shore.
The rabbits pause, they want to play,
In this wild place where we hide away.

Giggling Streams and Winking Flowers

By bubbling brooks, the daisies sway,
They twitch and wink, as if to say.
With every ripple, laughter flows,
In these bright fields, joy overflows.

The butterflies join in the spree,
Their flutters add to our glee.
We race the breeze, and what a sight,
As petals dance in pure delight.

Jubilant Jests of the Underbrush

The bushes rustle, secrets tell,
A fox pops out, and we all yell!
He playfully darts, a prankster spry,
As we fall down with laughter high.

A turtle stumbles, takes a slide,
We chuckle and cheer, such a wild ride!
In nature's court, the jesters reign,
With every giggle, we're free of pain.

The Joyous Heartbeat of the Hills

Laughter echoes in the breeze,
A hilltop dance with silly knees,
Flowers tickle our happy toes,
Joy leaps high, and never slows.

The rabbits waltz on sunlit paths,
Chasing shadows, sharing laughs,
Butterflies in goofy flight,
Spin around, oh what a sight!

Whimsy in the Woodland Whisper

Trees nod their heads in jolly cheer,
Squirrels play tag, without a fear,
Leaves rustle with a cheeky grin,
Nature's stage, let the fun begin!

A fox in socks prances with flair,
Twirling round without a care,
Mushrooms giggle like childhood dreams,
In moonlit glades, the laughter beams.

Glee Beneath the Towering Trees

Under branches that softly sway,
A band of critters starts to play,
Raccoons juggle acorns with glee,
While owls hoot in harmony!

Sunlight dances through the leaves,
Weave in the joy that nature weaves,
Each rustling leaf a hilarious song,
Join the fun, you can't go wrong!

Sprouting Joy in Every Corner

In every nook where sunshine spills,
Laughter grows like daffodils,
Caterpillars spinning tales anew,
As daisies nodding, join the crew!

Bouncing beetles with a jazzy beat,
Singing songs that are oh-so-sweet,
A garden party of pure delight,
Laughter shines, from day to night!

Grins Under the Greenery

Beneath the leaves, a squirrel spun,
Chasing shadows, oh what fun!
A garden gnome with a silly hat,
Stood frozen still, as a cat crept past.

The flowers dance in a gentle breeze,
Tickling toes of busy bees.
A rabbit hops with a joyful leap,
While nearby, a worm falls fast asleep.

Chuckles in the Canopy

A parrot squawks a silly tune,
While critters gather under the moon.
The branches sway with each little jig,
A dancing fern with a joyful wig.

Rustling leaves hide giggles and snorts,
As little frogs play hop and court.
A playful breeze brings chuckles anew,
While fireflies twinkle, just for a view.

The Raucous Rhythms of the Forest

In the woods, the rhythm's alive,
Woodpeckers drum to the jive.
A dancing fox in a bright bowtie,
Makes the owls hoot as they fly by.

The brook bubbles with laughter so clear,
While a deer prances without any fear.
Squirrels debate on a branch up high,
Sharing jokes that make them all sigh.

Joyful Jaunts Through the Pines

Through towering pines, the giggles race,
A chorus of critters fill the space.
With every step, there's a twist and a turn,
Where laughter flows, and fun will churn!

The sunbeams peek through the branches tight,
While raccoons plan their next late-night fright.
A bunny bounces, a playful sport,
As laughter echoes from the woodland court.

Whispers from the Leafy Laughter

In the woods where shadows play,
Trees giggle bright, in their own way.
Squirrels toss their acorn hats,
While birds crack jokes and share their chats.

A breeze of chuckles sways the leaves,
Jokes dance among the rustling eaves.
Each branch a friend, each root a rhyme,
Chasing laughter, stealing time.

The Joyful Green Mosaic

A patchwork quilt of giggling greens,
Paints the forest with silly scenes.
Frogs leap high with a hopeful croak,
While flowers giggle, tickled by smoke.

Lamb's ears flop as they dance around,
Spinning tales without a sound.
Sunlight glimmers, winks with glee,
Nature's stage for all to see.

Sprigs of Smiles in the Breeze

A rustle here, a chuckle there,
Soft whispers float in the air.
The daisies cheer with their sunny cheer,
As laughter rings from ear to ear.

Breeze tickles cheeks, a playful tease,
As tiny ants march with such ease.
With every step, a giggle sprout,
In nature's joy, there is no doubt.

Laughter in the Canopy

High above in branches tall,
The canopy sings a merry call.
Monkeys swing with a silly shout,
As giggling leaves twist about.

The sun winks down with a knowing smile,
Nature's humor stretches a mile.
With every rustle, the laughter grows,
In every whisper, joy overflows.

Rhapsody of the Raindrops

Raindrops fall like little clowns,
Bouncing off old sleepy towns.
Puddles form with silly splashes,
Dancing feet in joyful hashes.

Umbrellas flip like open wings,
As laughter bursts from silly things.
Every drop a tiny tease,
Bringing smiles with playful ease.

Tittering Twigs and Leaves

Twigs are whispering jokes all day,
Leaves are chuckling in a sway.
Branches stretch with giddy glee,
Nature's giggles, wild and free.

Breezes carry chuckles wide,
As squirrels scamper, eyes open wide.
In the chorus of the trees,
Every sound's a laugh, a tease.

Grinning with the Greenery

Greens are laughing, bright and bold,
Tales of joy in leaves retold.
Flowers wink with bright, sweet scents,
Cheerful bands in nature's tents.

In the garden, giggles grow,
Sunlight dances, puts on a show.
Petals flutter, all in jest,
Wild and funny, nature's best.

Joy's Tapestry Among the Trees

Beneath the boughs, the stories spin,
Laughter echoes from within.
Kites hover, twisting in the air,
While branches play with gentle care.

Each rustle holds a secret joke,
Whispers shared amidst the oak.
Nature's laughter, soft and sweet,
A tapestry of joy to greet.

Foliage of Fun

In the trees, a squirrel prances,
Chasing shadows, taking chances.
Laughter echoes in the air,
Leaves dance gently, unaware.

The branches sway, a silly tune,
While birds play tricks, 'neath the moon.
Nature's stage, a happy play,
Where smiles bloom, come what may.

Cheer in the Conifers

Pine cones drop like little bombs,
Tickling toes in nature's palms.
Tree trunks wear a goofy grin,
While the bushes burst in spin.

Raccoons peek with masked delight,
Stirring giggles in the night.
Silly critters in a dance,
Invite you in for a chance.

Giggling with the Grass

The blades of green are tickled pink,
Giggling softly as we wink.
Dancing gently in the breeze,
Making mischief with such ease.

Ladybugs wear tiny hats,
As butterflies tease and chat.
With every rustle, every sound,
The laughter echoes all around.

The Joyful Journey Through the Green

Winding paths where chuckles hide,
Running wild, with joy as guide.
The path is lined with smiles spry,
As clouds above play peek-a-bye.

Through the foliage, giggles soar,
Nature's jesters, can't ignore.
With every step, joy's refrain,
In this green world, none in vain.

Laughter's Harmony in Nature's Choir

In the green, the critters play,
Chasing shadows, night and day.
Squirrels dance with leaps so spry,
While rabbits giggle, oh so high.

In the trees, the birds converse,
With melodies that can disperse.
A frog hops in, his voice a croak,
Creating laughter, oh what a joke!

The brook joins in with bubbling glee,
While bees buzz tunes—oh let it be!
Sunlight spills, a vibrant hue,
As daisies sway, they laugh anew.

Nature's laughter fills the air,
A song that banishes all despair.
Join the frolic, feel the cheer,
In this place, there's nothing to fear.

Whimsical Whispers in the Wilderness

In the forest, secrets dwell,
Trees share stories they can't tell.
Mice in suits play cards at night,
While owls hoot with pure delight.

Dancing leaves in twirling flight,
Twinkle under the silver light.
A babbling brook plays peek-a-boo,
While flowers chuckle, bright as dew.

Bunnies prance with floppy ears,
Chasing down their giggling fears.
Every rustle brings a smile,
In this land, let's stay a while.

Laughter echoes, wild and bold,
The whispers of the woods unfold.
Join the party, night or day,
In nature's whimsy, come and play!

Giggles on the Forest Floor

Mushrooms wear their caps with pride,
Crickets chirp, they can't abide.
Dirt and leaves beneath our feet,
Hide the chuckles, oh so sweet.

A hedgehog rolls with all its might,
And tumbles down, what a sight!
The ants parade in funny lines,
Marching onward, crossing pines.

Twigs snap under frolicsome paws,
As playful critters draw applause.
Every turn brings joy to chase,
In this secret, happy place.

Laughter springs from roots and ground,
In this woodland, glee is found.
Join the game, no need to soar,
Come and giggle on the floor!

The Delight of the Dappled Sun

Sunbeams dance through leafy crowns,
Lighting up the joyful towns.
Every stalk, a ticklish beam,
In nature's play, all share a dream.

Butterflies with painted wings,
Flutter by with giggling flings.
Hopping bugs on paths of light,
Bring the whimsy, pure delight.

The sun dips low, with golden rays,
Turning dull into a blaze.
Laughter wraps like warm embrace,
In this dreamy, sunny space.

With each twinkle, let hearts soar,
In the magic we explore.
Join the dance, let spirits run,
In the bliss of dappled sun!

Delightful Dances of the Spruce

In the forest, trees sway bright,
Swaying left, then swaying right.
Squirrels leap, then take a bow,
Nature's stage, a grand wow!

Frisky foxes join the play,
Chasing shadows, come what may.
Under branches, laughter roams,
Each step wiggles like gnome's homes.

Breezes hum a cheerful tune,
Dancing leaves, a bright festoon.
Even birds commence their cheer,
Singing tales for all to hear.

Glorious Gleams of Green

In meadows lush, the colors pop,
Dandelions giggle, never stop.
Butterflies flutter, oh what fun,
Chasing each other, all on the run.

Frogs leap high from lily pads,
Shimmering smiles, no room for sads.
Sunshine splashes on their skin,
Playful prances, let the games begin.

Dewdrops sparkle, morning face,
Making mischief, a light embrace.
In the green, the world's aglow,
Endless laughter, a vibrant show.

Laughter Beneath the Birch

Beneath the branches, giggles spill,
Rustling leaves, buzzing with thrill.
Ants march in a parade so grand,
Carrying crumbs, their tiny band.

With every breeze, jokes come alive,
Whispers from the trees, oh what a jive!
Silly shadows play peek-a-boo,
Nature's laughter, ever anew.

A squirrel sneezes, oh what a sound,
Echoing life all around.
Bouncing boughs in comedic sway,
Birch trees laugh the day away.

Tickled by the Willow

Willow branches scrape the sky,
Tickling clouds as they float by.
Waves of laughter in the stream,
Nature's jesters in a dream.

Crickets chirp in rhythmic cheer,
Adding their voice for all to hear.
Fireflies twinkle, playing tricks,
Lighting up the night with flicks.

Water ripples join the fun,
Reflections dance, one by one.
In this realm where giggles bloom,
Joyful spirits chase the gloom.

Joyful Encounters in the Underbrush

In the thicket, squirrels dance,
Chasing shadows with a glance.
Bouncing off each leafy floor,
Laughter echoes evermore.

Bunnies hop around the bend,
Sharing secrets with a friend.
A fox grins with a cheeky flair,
As butterflies float in the air.

The hedgehog's laugh is quite a sight,
Making mischief day and night.
At dusk, crickets start to sing,
Underneath the trees, they swing.

In this realm where joy is free,
Nature's winks bring glee to be.
Each encounter, bright and bold,
In the underbrush, fun unfolds.

Charmed Giggles of the Glade

In the glade where daisies sway,
A band of frogs begins to play.
With tiny hats and banjos tight,
They croak their tunes into the night.

Twinkling lights like fireflies,
Guide the revelry that flies.
Each bloom shakes with laughter loud,
Beneath a moon that feels so proud.

The owls hoot a curious cheer,
Adding whimsy to the sphere.
A raccoon with a playful wink,
Snags a snack and starts to drink.

In the glade, joy reigns supreme,
Charmed by nature's playful dream.
Each giggle springs from roots so deep,
In this wonder, we all leap.

The Lighthearted Lullaby of Leaves

Whispering softly, leaves take flight,
  Tickling whispers, day and night.
  Singing songs with rustling cheer,
    Nature's giggles fill the sphere.

  Squirrels chase with giddy twirls,
While the breeze sends tails in swirls.
  Each drop of dew laughs in glee,
  As sunlight plays among the trees.

The branches sway, they dip and dive,
   Creating joy where all contrive.
    In this lull, a cheeky breeze,
Brings forth smiles with playful ease.

  Oh, the tales that leaves will spin,
 With cheeky grins and laughter's din.
    Every flutter hints of fun,
   In a world where joy is spun.

Revelry in the Rustic Realm

In the rustic realm, a dance begins,
Where humor sparks and joy never thins.
A goat with bells hops round and round,
While all the critters gather 'round.

The chickens join with a cluck and a cheer,
As piglets roll in the mud without fear.
The sun dips low, the shadows grow,
In this laughter-filled show, they steal the glow.

A hedgehog leads with a twig in hand,
Creating chaos, lively and grand.
The laughter rings beneath the trees,
Where joy is spread by the softest breeze.

Revelry blooms where smiles ignite,
In this rustic realm, pure delight.
Every heartbeat sways with the tune,
Under the watchful eyes of the moon.

Rooted Revelries in the Meadow

In the meadow, laughter sings,
A frog wears shoes and flaps his wings.
Butterflies dance, twirling about,
While daisies giggle, there's no doubt.

A rabbit juggles, oh what a sight,
With carrots flying, oh what a fright!
The sun peeks in, a grin on its face,
As clouds join in this hilarious race.

The breeze tells jokes to the waving grass,
Tickling the daisies as they all laugh.
A squirrel spins tales from branch to branch,
In this meadow, there's always a chance.

So leave your worries, just take a seat,
Join the laughter, feel the upbeat.
In this rooted revelry, all is bright,
Where joy and whimsy dance in daylight.

Tickling Blooms and Cheerful Coos

Oh, the flowers, bright and bold,
Tell secrets that never grow old.
A hummingbird hums a tune so sweet,
While tulips bob, they can't be beat.

Daffodils giggle under tall trees,
As a chubby bee buzzes with ease.
The sparrows chirp, a comic refrain,
In this garden, fun's never plain.

Butterflies swirl in a dizzying dance,
While ladybugs plot their next prance.
The wind whispers tales of lighthearted glee,
In this vibrant world, so wild and free.

Tickling blooms in cheerful affray,
Invite all to join the joyful play.
So gather 'round, let laughter grow,
In nature's embrace, let happiness flow.

The Whimsy of Winding Trails

Along the trails where shadows prance,
A turtle dares to take a chance.
With a hat on his head, he moves so slow,
He's the king of the path, don't you know?

A squirrel slides down with a happy squeak,
While frogs in the creeks play hide and seek.
The flowers wave, they know what to do,
They dance in the wind, just like me and you.

At every turn, there's something to see,
A puffy cloud that looks like a bee.
The giggling brook runs wide and free,
Spreading chuckles as far as can be.

So come take a stroll on these winding trails,
Where whimsy reigns and laughter prevails.
Every footstep echoes with delight,
In nature's carnival, everything feels right.

Silly Shadows Against the Bark

Silly shadows dance on the bark,
Playing games in the brightening dark.
A raccoon winks as he scampers by,
Under a moon that chuckles in the sky.

Owls hoot jokes from their leafy perch,
While fireflies flicker in a merry search.
The woods are alive with playful delight,
As mischief unfolds in soft, silver light.

Trees sway gently, joining the fun,
With branches that twist and hearts that run.
Each crack of a twig brings whispers of cheer,
A raucous symphony that all can hear.

So if you wander 'neath this starlit cloak,
Join the shadows in laughter and poke.
For in this forest, with a heart that's stark,
Silly shadows weave joy against the bark.

Soft Giggles in the Glade

In a glade where shadows play,
The rabbits dance, hip-hip-hooray!
With a wiggle and a woosh,
They make the flowers blush and swoosh.

A squirrel spins in wobbly twirls,
Chasing bouncy acorn pearls.
Each tumble brings a cheerful cheer,
While frolicsome friends bring joy near.

The wind whispers through the leaves,
Tickling noses, making thieves
Of laughter, spry and light as air,
A giggle fest, without a care.

So in this glade, where giggles rise,
The sunbeams dance beneath the skies.
Together we'll share in this fun,
With silly tales for everyone!

Whimsy in the Willow

Beneath the willow's swaying dress,
A puppy spins in pure excess.
With each bark, the branches sway,
In a game of hide and play.

The gentle breeze begins to tease,
As bees do balance on the trees.
They hum their tunes, a merry hum,
While pastel petals start to come.

A chipmunk with a cap on tight,
Launches nuts with all his might.
Each thud a giggle, much delight,
As friends come rushing at first sight.

With laughter ringing all around,
Joy is found where friends abound.
Each moment here, a precious thrill,
In the heart of the willow still!

Grinning in the Glens

In the glen where giggles roam,
A hedgehog rolls, his spines like foam.
With each plop, he makes quite funny,
Chasing sunbeams, oh so sunny!

The bunnies hop, their ears so long,
They dance in circles, twirling strong.
With every leap, a snicker shared,
In this joyous place, no one is scared.

A raccoon with a twinkle eye,
Steals a snack and gives a sigh.
With sticky fingers, what a scene,
His happy antics, always keen.

So in the glens where laughter's found,
We're grinning wide, joy knows no bound.
A pocket full of mirth today,
In cheerful tunes, we sing and play!

A Symphony of Smiles

In the park where laughter blends,
A symphony, where joy transcends.
With every chuckle, a note does rise,
A melody bright beneath the skies.

The sunbeams giggle as they shine,
Tickling flowers, oh so divine.
The birds join in with songs of cheer,
Painting the air with notes sincere.

A dance of shadows, twirls abound,
Beneath the trees, on grassy ground.
Each smile exchanged, a treasured score,
Brings life alive, we want more!

So gather 'round, both young and old,
In this symphony, tales unfold.
With every laugh, a bond we seal,
In the concert of joy, we all feel!

Nature's Playful Palette

Colors dance upon the stream,
A brush of joy, a vivid dream.
The flowers giggle, petals sway,
In sunny hues, they laugh and play.

Bubbly brooks and chirping birds,
Nature's laughter, without words.
The trees don hats of grassy green,
In this realm, all's bright and clean.

Bouncing bunnies chase their tails,
With wiggles, hops, and funny trails.
Butterflies join in the jive,
Winking at the bees alive.

So let us cheer with nature's art,
In every leaf, a joyful heart.
The laughter echoes, wild and free,
As whimsical as a budding tree.

Gleeful Echoes Amidst the Green

Whispers chuckle through the trees,
As branches sway in playful breeze.
A squirrel rolls and spins in glee,
    Nature's jest, a sight to see.

The daisies nod, they know the joke,
While crickets chirp, a merry croak.
The sunlight tickles grassy beds,
Where shadows dance upon our heads.

In hidden spots, the laughter sprouts,
With all the chirping, there's no doubt.
A frolicsome breeze fluffs the leaves,
    Tickles and jiggles, how it weaves!

So let's play tag, out in the sun,
With joyful hearts, we'll always run.
Among the green, where spirits see,
    The playfulness of harmony.

The Rapture of the Roots

Roots beneath share silly tales,
Of wandering ants and windy gales.
The dirt erupts with laughter's sound,
As thriving life springs from the ground.

The mushrooms giggle in a patch,
While toadstools play a little match.
Inside the soil, secrets churn,
With every twist, the humor burns.

Frogs play leapfrog by the stream,
Their jumps are part of nature's dream.
In mud-streaked suits, they take their chance,
To hop along, and laugh, and prance.

So listen close, for roots impart,
The joy of land, the song of heart.
Beneath our feet, a world so wide,
Wonders hide where smiles abide.

Grinning Sunbeams Through the Trees

Sunbeams streak, a giggling light,
Dancing through branches, warm and bright.
Where shadows play and whispers cheer,
A symphony of joy appears.

With every ray, the world ignites,
In pastel hues, the day delights.
Birds jest above with songs so sweet,
Barefoot adventures guide our feet.

The breezes tease, a playful friend,
They swirl and laugh, their smiles extend.
Underneath the leafy show,
Nature's fun, a vibrant flow.

So join the frolic, let it be,
Feel the laughter, wild and free.
In every glimmer, life's embrace,
A tender smile, a friendly space.

Mischief in the Maple Leaves

In the trees the squirrels play,
Chasing tails and leaves away.
A hidden acorn causes glee,
As they dance with such esprit.

Rabbits hop without a care,
While the birds just sing and share.
A mischief maker flicks his tail,
As laughter rings with every fail.

On a branch, a chipmunk grins,
Tickling friends with swirling spins.
Down below, the laughter swells,
Life's a joke, as nature tells.

Golden sunbeams shine so bright,
Filling hearts with pure delight.
In the woods, with friends we stay,
Mischief rules our lively play.

Dancing Shadows of Delight

Underneath the swaying trees,
Whispers float upon the breeze.
Shadows twist and turn around,
As giggles echo, joy abound.

Footsteps light on grassy ground,
A cheerful hop can soon be found.
Sunbeams flicker in our eyes,
Hidden jokes and sweet surprise.

With each leap, a laughter burst,
In this moment, joy's dispersed.
A playful dance, a silly pose,
In our hearts, the laughter grows.

Chasing shadows, feeling free,
A world of fun, just you and me.
The sun bows down, the day draws near,
With every chuckle, we have no fear.

Laughter in the Old Oak

Beneath the old oak, stories flow,
Where playful winds begin to blow.
Squirrels chatter, branches sway,
Laughter dances through the day.

Picnics laid without a care,
Spread delight that we all share.
Cookies vanish with a cheer,
As friends bring snacks and brightened gear.

A gentle breeze tugs on my hat,
While someone shouts, "Come chase the cat!"
With a rush and gleeful shout,
We tumble down, no room for doubt.

In the shade, we rest and play,
Telling tales in a silly way.
With each laugh, we bond anew,
Under the oak, our joy is true.

Breezy Chuckles Under the Sun

The sun is bright, the sky is blue,
Breezy giggles chase us too.
A kite soars high, then dips and glides,
While we squeal with joy beside.

Picnic blankets laid on green,
Sandwiches hide in the scene.
Someone trips, their drink takes flight,
And laughter bursts in pure delight.

A gentle race, a friendly fight,
Chasing shadows feels just right.
With every tumble, joy will swell,
As hearts ring loud with laughter's bell.

Kites and laughter fill the day,
With sunny skies that seem to say,
In this moment, we are found,
Joyful chuckles all around.

Nature's Quiet Chuckle

In the woods where shadows play,
Trees tell jokes in their own way.
Squirrels snicker in the breeze,
While flowers giggle, whispering leaves.

The brook hums a silly tune,
Under the gaze of a lazy moon.
Frogs join in with a croaky air,
As crickets chirp without a care.

Bunnies bounce with a hop and a skip,
Chasing butterflies, a merry trip.
Laughter echoes through the glade,
In nature's fun, we're all charade.

So when you wander through the green,
Listen closely, feel the sheen.
For every chuckle, every cheer,
Nature's humor is ever near.

Sunlit Sprouts and Merry Melodies

Amidst the blooms, the sunbeams dance,
Each petal sways, a little prance.
Buds laugh as they burst and grow,
In a garden of jokes, what a show!

The daisies wink, the roses tease,
Comical whispers carried by the breeze.
Bees buzz jokes, giggling in flight,
While ladybugs roll with pure delight.

Mushrooms chuckle in their caps,
Telling tales of funny mishaps.
With every sprout, there's joy to find,
In sunlit corners, laughter entwined.

So gather round and share the cheer,
Leave your worries far and near.
With every bloom and every smile,
Nature's laughter makes it all worthwhile.

Fables of the Forest Frolic

Once in a forest, wild and bright,
Creatures gathered, a sheer delight.
Foxes grinned with mischievous eyes,
Squirrels tumbled, drawing surprise.

Owls hooted quirky little rhymes,
While chipmunks chattered, all in chimes.
The woodpecker had a pun or two,
As each critter chimed in the fun zoo.

Tales of mischief floated through trees,
Of raccoons sneaking snacks with ease.
Laughter danced on every branch,
In tales of friendship, all took a chance.

So join the frolic, let spirits soar,
In this fabled forest, who could ask for more?
With every giggle, the stories swell,
In nature's heart, all is well.

Breezy Banter from the Boughs

High up in trees, the branches sway,
Leaves are laughing, come what may.
A parrot squawks a cheeky line,
While the sun sets with a golden shine.

The winds tell tales of days gone by,
As clouds chuckle, drifting by.
Each twig carries a playful tease,
From lively critters to buzzing bees.

A raccoon smirks with a shiny chest,
While squirrels perform their acrobatic jest.
In the heart of the forest, joy takes flight,
Each moment filled with pure delight.

So when you hear that breezy sound,
Know laughter lives all around.
In nature's circus, let's all play,
And bounce through life in a funny way.

Blithe Spirits in the Brush

In a thicket where laughter grows,
Squirrels dance in silly flows.
A hedgehog rolls with a comical frown,
While rabbits hop in a jolly gown.

A chatty bird with a bright green hat,
Tells the trees where to find the chat.
They giggle at the clouds passing by,
As butterflies flutter, oh my, oh my!

Down by the brook where the antics unfold,
Frogs compete in a leap, oh so bold!
With a plop and a splash, they cause quite a scene,
In this cheery world where all feel keen.

Laughter echoes through each merry glade,
In the heart of the woods where fun is played.
Join the frolic, join the cheer,
For joy in the brush is always near.

Merry Musings in the Meadow

Under the sun, a band of bees,
Buzzing along with giggles and glee.
They tickle the flowers, make daisies sneeze,
In this meadow of mirth, life's a tease.

Fluffy clouds like ticklish sheep,
Laze in the sky, in soft, gentle sleep.
While grasshoppers leap with a hop and a skip,
Chasing dreams on a whimsical trip.

A playful wind whispers sweet tricks,
Mixing colors of lollipop licks.
Frolicking nymphs in the shade of a tree,
Each giggle floats on a breezy spree.

Merriment reigns with each tiny breeze,
As daisies sway and dance with ease.
In this joyful spot where laughter will grow,
Come join the fun, let your spirit glow!

The Riddle of the Rustling Foliage

In rustling leaves, a riddle spins,
Where the laughter of nature begins.
A clever fox with a sly little wink,
Plays hide and seek in a puddle to drink.

The trees share jokes in a breezy tone,
While chipmunks giggle, not feeling alone.
A squirrel scampers with a nut on his head,
Chasing shadows that playfully spread.

Whispers of fun in the twinkling light,
As shadows dance and the heart feels bright.
A mystery hides in each giggle and chuckle,
In the foliage where joy will snuggle.

Follow the giggles, they lead the way,
To a spot where the wild things play.
In nature's riddle, let your heart soar,
For laughter unlocked is a timeless score.

Frolic in the Flowering Woods

Amidst the blooms, the frolic begins,
Where the scent of laughter sweetly spins.
Bouncing branches with colorful flare,
Invite all critters to come and share.

A merry deer with a jaunty stride,
Winks at a fox, who runs off to hide.
While butterflies orchestrate a dance,
With petals as partners, they twirl and prance.

In a sunny glade, a party unfolds,
With daffodils dressed in yellow-gold.
The grass whispers jokes as the breeze goes by,
Tickling the noses of squirrels nearby.

The woods, alive with joyous delight,
Celebrate laughter from morning to night.
Come join the fun, let your spirit soar,
In this frolicsome realm, forever explore!

Gentle Guffaws of the Grove

In a forest where whispers play,
Trees chuckle at the end of the day.
Squirrels dance with nutty glee,
While branches sway in jubilee.

A deer trips over a fallen log,
And owls laugh as they survey the fog.
The wind teases leaves, causing a stir,
Each rustle is a giggle, a cheerful blur.

Beneath the bark, the beetles sing,
Tickling the roots in a joyful fling.
Sunlight dapples through leafy crowns,
Nature chuckles, wearing crowns of browns.

So in this grove of laughter's birth,
Find silly moments, it's pure mirth.
With every step, wear a grin,
For laughter is the sweetest win!

The Sprightly Song of the Savanna

Blades of grass sway to the beat,
Hopping critters tap their feet.
The sun shines bright, oh what a sight,
As zebras prance in pure delight.

A giraffe snickers, munching high,
While lion cubs chase clouds in the sky.
Cheetahs slide in playful runs,
Every chase brings hearty puns.

Around the baobab, friends unite,
Each shadow giggles, pure dynamite.
Moments shared beneath the sun,
Savanna laughs, a world of fun.

With every rustle, hear the cheer,
From playful hearts that gather here.
In this land where joy's in season,
Every smile has its own reason!

Pleased With Each Petal's Tease

Daisies peek from the green so bright,
Tickling bees with pure delight.
Butterflies dance, oh what a show,
In this floral land where giggles flow.

Tulips wave their colors bold,
Whispering secrets, stories told.
A rose gets shy, its petals blush,
As daisies laugh, there's quite a hush.

Sun-kissed petals, a playful tease,
Each brings whispers upon the breeze.
With every bloom, laughter's sound,
Nature's chuckle is all around.

In gardens where joy takes its stance,
Petals twirl in a merry dance.
So come and play, feel the ease,
With every smile, you'll find the keys!

Laughter among the Wildflowers

Wildflowers giggle in fields so wide,
Hosting parties where critters abide.
Bumblebees buzz with silly rhymes,
Chasing joy through sunlit climes.

A plucky rabbit with floppy ears,
Jumps around, spreading cheers.
Grasshoppers leap in sprightly bounds,
While laughter echoes through the grounds.

With petals bright, and colors rare,
Joyful whispers fill the air.
Every breeze brings a playful sigh,
As nature joins the laughter high.

In this wildflower patch so free,
Laughter dances with jubilee.
Join the fun beneath the skies,
Where every giggle surely flies!

The Brightness of Nature's Grin

In the garden where flowers sway,
Butterflies dance and children play.
There's a monkey in a tree, so spry,
With a silly hat, oh my, oh my!

A squirrel chuckles, quick on its feet,
Chasing shadows, what a treat!
With acorns tossed in playful flight,
Nature's jesters dance in delight.

The sun peeks out with a cheeky glare,
As if it's part of the joyful affair.
Raindrops giggle upon the ground,
In this happy world, laughter's found.

So come and join this merry spree,
Where nature holds the best jubilee.
With smiles and grins, joy will arise,
In the brightness under sunny skies.

Lively Loops of Lush Landscapes

Around the bend, the meadows laugh,
In fields of green, all is daft.
With daisies wearing crowns of sun,
They sway and sway, oh what fun!

The laughing brook sings silly tunes,
Beneath the gaze of cuddly moons.
With wiggles and giggles on every shore,
It splashes joy, forevermore.

A gopher pops up, a grin so wide,
It digs and dances, full of pride.
The trees are swaying, a funny dance,
In this cheerful land, all take a chance.

So skip along the winding trails,
Where every step ignites the gales.
In lively loops, let your heart soar,
With the land's laughter, we'll always explore.

Laughter Among the Pines

Among the pines, a chatter glows,
As laughter rises where the wind blows.
A chipmunk juggles at the foot of a tree,
While squirrels join in, as happy as can be.

The gales giggle and tickle the leaves,
Creating chuckles that dance in eves.
With shadows stretching, they tease and play,
In such a merry, delightful array.

A fox tells tales with a wink and a grin,
As rabbits hop forth, ready to join in.
Under the stars, the fun won't end,
In this joyful valley, where all friends blend.

So let your laughter echo through the night,
Among the pines, everything feels right.
With nature's jokes and playful scenes,
We celebrate life, just like queens and kings.

Whispers of the Forest

In the forest deep, whispers arise,
With secrets shared 'neath sapphire skies.
A woodpecker tapping in a funny beat,
Makes the whole place feel light on its feet.

Bushes rustle with giggles and charm,
While bunnies hop by, causing no harm.
Each leaf holds a giggle, a playful quirk,
In this joyful retreat, where spirits lurk.

The owls chuckle in the dusky light,
Casting silly shadows that dance in flight.
With whispers echoing through branches high,
Nature's laughter makes the world sigh.

So listen closely to the forest's cheer,
In playful whispers that draw us near.
Every giggle, each snicker, they blend,
In the quietude where wonders extend.

Jests of the Juniper

A juniper spoke with a witty flair,
It shared silly tales in the crisp, cool air.
With every giggle, the branches would sway,
Dancing with laughter, brightening the day.

The squirrels all chuckled while munching on seeds,
They rolled on the ground, laughing at weeds.
The sun peeked out, tickling the leaves,
As nature joined in, it's hard not to believe.

The Swaying Serenade

The trees sang a tune with a jig and a twist,
Each note brought a chuckle, a grin to persist.
Breezes would tickle the trunks as they danced,
The laughter of branches—the joy was enhanced.

A woodpecker rhythmically tapped along,
While the rabbits hopped in a merry old song.
The shadows grew long with each silly quip,
Nature's own humor—a delightful trip.

Glee Beneath the Boughs

Beneath all the bows where the sunlight beams,
The critters exchanged their most humorous schemes.
The shadows played tricks, they danced on the ground,
As giggles erupted from all around.

A raccoon cracked jokes while a fox rolled with glee,
The chorus of laughter rang wild and free.
In this silly green realm where the banter took flight,
The joy stretched for miles, oh, what a delight!

Cheerful Echoes in the Timber

Echoes of laughter would bounce through the trees,
Tickling the trunks with a soft, playful breeze.
A porcupine quipped, "I'm prickly but fun!"
While a wise old owl winked, "Let's all be one!"

The jovial whispers weaved tales sweet and bright,
Nature was buzzing, a festival of light.
A symphony of smiles, a chorus of cheer,
In the woodland's embrace, oh, happiness near!

The Merriment of Mistletoe

Beneath the boughs, we dance and sway,
With silly hats that bounce away.
Laughter rings like jingle bells,
In joyful tales, our friendship dwells.

A squirrel dons a tiny scarf,
While woodland critters giggle and laugh.
A snowman winks, his carrot nose,
As everyone strikes a silly pose.

Mistletoe glimmers, mischief in tow,
Under its charm, we steal the show.
In every corner, chuckles explode,
A party of joy down this festive road.

Enchanted Echoes Beneath the Fir

Beneath the fir, where shadows play,
Whispers of pranks float on the sway.
Dancing lights twinkle, up high and bright,
Chasing each other till late at night.

A raccoon with a top hat spins,
While gnomes pull sneaky little grins.
Silly secrets shared in delight,
As giggles echo with pure delight.

The owls hoot in playful refrain,
In this woodland, joy is our gain.
Laughter sparkles like stars above,
A symphony made of pure fun and love.

The Happy Heart of the Woods

In the heart of woods, a party brews,
With chipmunk flair and dazzling views.
A dance-off starts, the beat takes flight,
As creatures twirl under moonlit night.

Frogs croak jokes while badgers clap,
Each twist and turn deserves a clap.
Squirrels tumble, a sight to behold,
In this patch of joy, we're never old.

The pine trees sway with easy grace,
As mischief finds its favorite place.
Every chuckle bounces around,
In this happy heart, love knows no bound.

Playtime in the Palms

In the palms where the sun beams down,
Laughter rises above the town.
A monkey cracks jokes, swinging high,
While parrots burst with colors sly.

Belly flops splash in shimmering waves,
Every leap a tale of brave knaves.
Crabs play tag on sandy shore,
As giggles erupt, who could ask for more?

Sunsets dance with hues that burst,
In this playground, we always thirst.
For laughter shared, in every fling,
We find the joy that only fun can bring.

Radiant Robins and Raucous Riddles

In the garden, robins play,
Chasing shadows that dance away.
With a hop and a cheerful cheep,
They make us laugh, their joy so deep.

Silly squirrels in a nutty chase,
Up the tree, they zigzag in grace.
Tumbling down with a little squeak,
Their antics leave us all so weak.

A wily fox with a sly little grin,
Sneaks through the bushes, ready to win.
He trips on roots and rolls with glee,
The funniest critter there ever could be.

Under the sun, laughter is sound,
Where nature's joy is always found.
With every giggle, the day feels bright,
In this lively world, oh what a sight!

Chortles Among the Pines

Beneath the pines, a chuckle grows,
A flurry of leaves where laughter flows.
Rabbits hop with a wiggle and wag,
While a sneaky raccoon makes off with a rag.

Squirrels gossip over acorn schemes,
Crafting plans like mischievous dreams.
With a leap and a spin, they twirl in delight,
Their raucous laughter echoes through the night.

Woodpeckers knock, creating a beat,
Join the fun, don't miss a seat!
The forest is vibrant with silly, sweet sounds,
In this wild wood, joy knows no bounds.

Each cackle and giggle wraps around trees,
A symphony played by the buzzing bees.
Laughter erupts as the sun starts to sink,
In the heart of the woods, let's swirl and think!

The Playful Dance of Nature

Butterflies flutter in a joyful ballet,
Spinning and twirling, come join the play.
A dance of colors, oh what a sight,
In the garden's embrace, everything feels right.

Wiggly worms in a writhing line,
Twirling and stretching, oh so fine.
They wiggle with joy beneath the sun's glow,
Nature's own dancers, putting on a show.

Here comes a dog, paws pattering loud,
Chasing his tail, he's laughing, so proud.
With a tumble and bark, he joins the spree,
In this merry world, how happy we be!

Clouds above drift like fluffy dreams,
Tickling the trees and dancing in beams.
Together we giggle, a symphonic cheer,
In the playful dance, we lose all fear.

Harmony in the Hushed Woods

In the quiet woods where shadows play,
Whispers of laughter float, come what may.
A chorus of giggles fills the air,
As nature grins with an innocent flair.

A cheeky crow on a low-hanging limb,
Sings out a joke to the tree's leafy rim.
With raucous caws that echo and swell,
He shares a secret we know too well.

Beneath the boughs, a rabbit appears,
Wobbling along, it shakes off its fears.
With a hop and a skip, it tumbles around,
Creating a joy that knows no bound.

As day turns to dusk, the woods come alive,
With silly stories, the critters contrive.
In harmony, they find their sweet tune,
Under the glow of a chuckling moon.

The Joyful Grove

In a grove where laughter rings,
Trees dance, and the sparrow sings.
Squirrels play a game of tag,
While a wise old owl looks and brags.

Breezes tickle leafy cheeks,
Sunlight plays, and mischief peaks.
A bunny hops with silly flair,
Chasing shadows without a care.

Laughter lingers in the air,
Tickling noses everywhere.
The flowers giggle, colors bright,
Twinkling like stars at night.

In this grove, joy knows no bounds,
Magic sparkles on the grounds.
With every chuckle, trees sway soft,
A playful haven where hearts loft.

Chortling Through the Canopy

Above, the laughter echoes high,
As playful clouds drift by.
A chubby raccoon rolls on the ground,
In this canopy, joy is found.

Birds jest and flutter without a care,
Tickling leaves on limbs laid bare.
Singing songs of silly dreams,
In a world where humor beams.

Down below, the critters prance,
In the sunshine, they dance.
With every jump and quirky twist,
Not a moment goes amiss.

So join the fun beneath the trees,
Hear the laughter on the breeze.
Chortling through branches wide,
In nature's joy, we all abide.

Playful Breezes in the Woods

Whispers of giggles on the wind,
Nature's jesters, never pinned.
A breeze with tickles means delight,
With every swish, it takes flight.

Dancing petals mesmerize,
As butterflies wear funny ties.
A hidden gnome gives a wink,
In the woods, we all can think.

Squirrels scatter, making haste,
As they nibble on their taste.
With a hop and a playful jive,
Life in the woods feels so alive.

So let your spirit laugh and soar,
Through leafy lanes and nature's door.
With playful breezes and sunny cheer,
In these woods, there's nothing to fear.

Songs from the Green Heart

In the heart of the woods, a song plays,
Filling the air in delightful ways.
Whimsical echoes of joy abound,
While nature's melodies swirl around.

A playful frog croaks a cheerful tune,
Bouncing beneath the laughing moon.
With every note, the critters sway,
Creating smiles that brighten the day.

Rustling leaves share their secrets sweet,
In the midst of frolic, they skip a beat.
The brook bubbles with joyous glee,
As it joins in this symphony.

From the thrumming heart of the green,
A vibrant world is clearly seen.
So dance to the laughter, sing with might,
In nature's concert, hearts feel light.

www.ingramcontent.com/pod-product-compliance
Lightning Source LLC
Chambersburg PA
CBHW072145200426
43209CB00051B/566